Get Set Go ✦ Mathematics

Numbers 1-10

Miles Kelly

About the consultant

Experienced Key Stage 1 and Key Stage 2 teacher Caroline Clissold is passionate about raising standards in mathematics teaching in primary schools. She was a consultant and regional co-ordinator for the National Centre for Excellence in the Teaching of Mathematics, delivers in-service training for a specialist mathematics education publisher, supports teaching and learning in various schools, and has guest lectured at a number of London universities. Her aim is to increase children's enjoyment of mathematics, helping them to see purpose in their learning. She strongly believes in a creative approach to teaching so that children can use and apply maths skills in meaningful contexts.

First published in 2020 by Miles Kelly Publishing Ltd
Harding's Barn, Bardfield End Green, Thaxted, Essex, CM6 3PX, UK

Copyright © Miles Kelly Publishing Ltd 2020

2 4 6 8 10 9 7 5 3 1

Publishing Director Belinda Gallagher
Creative Director Jo Cowan
Editorial Director Rosie Neave
Managing Designer Joe Jones
Designer Venita Kidwai
Illustrators Ailie Busby, Maddie Frost
Production Elizabeth Collins, Jennifer Brunwin-Jones
Image Manager Liberty Newton
Reprographics Stephan Davis
Assets Lorraine King

ISBN 978-1-78989-100-3

Printed in China
British Library Cataloguing-in-Publication Data
A catalogue record for this book is available from the British Library

Made with paper from a sustainable forest

www.mileskelly.net

CONTENTS

Let's start practising!

1
2
3
4
5
6
7
8
9
10

Counting

...with The Three Billy Goats Gruff!

Draw along the dotted lines.

Introduction

Learning to count

According to researchers Gelman and Gallistel there are five main stages that children work through to master counting. The activities in this book explore the first four of these stages. The fifth stage requires practical exploration.

1. A child can count without knowing anything more than that there is an order in which the numbers are counted. At this stage, you should count items together, encouraging your child to learn this order.

2. A child will point to, for example, three items and as they touch each one, can say the number names 'one', 'two', 'three', matching each word with an item. This is known as one-to-one correspondence. If you ask them how many there are at this stage, it is common for the child to say a completely different (wrong) number.

3. A child understands that the last number said in one-to-one correspondence is the number that communicates how many there are in that particular group.

4. A child can tell you how many items there are when the same objects are rearranged, without counting them all over again.

5. A child can count items without looking. You can practice this stage by asking your child to listen (no peeking!) to the sound of you dropping up to 10 pennies into a cup one by one, and then asking them how many pennies are in the cup.

INSTRUCTION TEXT explains what your child will be learning on each spread and how to approach the activities

CHARACTER SPEECH provides extra activities, tips and guidance

1–5: H

Ask your count each ite each one as they you how many there to write the numer they start to rec help them to pr numerals b

How many
goats g

Counting to 10

Remember to point to each item as you count it.

How many bees?

How many clouds?

How many flowers?

36

...any are there?

At last the goats came to a bridge. On the other side they saw a lovely green meadow. "That looks yummy!" said the little billy goat gruff.

1 2 3 4 5

But a horrible troll lived under the bridge. He had big teeth, and he liked nothing better than goat for dinner!

How many trolls?

How many frogs?

How many apples?

How many lily pads?

Draw one more lily pad. How many can you see now?

Well done! 13

For more practice turn to page 32

STORY TEXT
keeps your child engaged and makes learning and practising fun

DOTTED LINES
to trace throughout help to improve pen control

TICKS
for your child to trace when they complete each spread provide an extra sense of achievement

6 7 8 9 10

How many trees?

How many butterflies?

Well done! 37

NUMERALS
strengthen the link between counting and the symbols that we use to express numbers, and can be traced when your child is ready to do so

ACTIVITIES
guide your child through the stages of learning to count, step by step

Counting in order to 5

Ask your child to count the items on this page with you. Point to each one as you count. Your child may not be able to point and count along with you yet.

Once upon a time there lived three billy goats gruff. They loved to eat grass all day long.

Can you count the **billy goats gruff?**

Can you count the **flowers?**

Can you count the **clouds?**

1 2 3 4 5

If our cousin Bobby was here too, how many goats would you see?

Can you count the **mountains**?

Can you count the **trees**?

For more practice turn to page 28

Well done!

9

1-5: Draw around and count

Ask your child to draw around each item they are asked to count below. Count each item aloud as they draw. Make sure that the number they say corresponds with the number they are circling.

One day the three goats couldn't find any grass to eat – they had eaten it all up! "Let's find some more," said the big billy goat gruff.

Can you count the **bees**?

Can you count the **birds**?

Can you count the **butterflies**?

The goats walked and walked. "Are we there yet?" asked the little billy goat gruff. "I'm starving!"

Can you count the **flowers**?

Can you count the **snails**?

For more practice turn to page 30

Well done!

1–5: How many are there?

Ask your child to count each item, pointing to each one as they go, and then to tell you how many there are. Show them how to write the numerals in the boxes so they start to recognize them, then help them to practise writing the numerals by themselves.

At last the goats came to a bridge. On the other side they saw a lovely green meadow. "That looks yummy!" said the little billy goat gruff.

How many billy goats gruff?

How many trolls?

How many frogs?

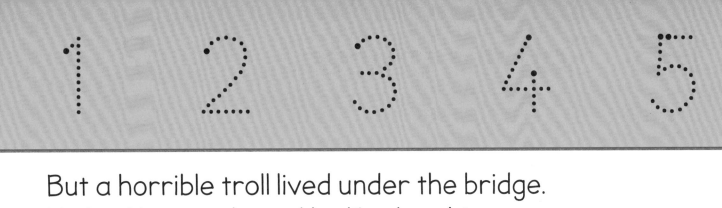

But a horrible troll lived under the bridge. He had big teeth, and he liked nothing better than goat for dinner!

How many **apples?**

How many **lily pads?**

Draw one more lily pad. How many can you see now?

For more practice turn to page 32

Well done!

13

1-5: Same number, looks different

Encourage your child to count the first set of each item. See if they can tell you how many there are in the second set without counting them, then write the correct numbers in the boxes.

The goats thought about all the delicious things they would eat when they crossed the bridge.

How many **apples?**

How many **apples?**

How many **flowers?**

How many **flowers?**

How many **leaves?**

How many **leaves?**

"I'll cross first," said the little billy goat gruff. He set off over the bridge.

Suddenly the troll jumped out. "Who is trip-trapping over my bridge?" he roared.

"Only me," said the little billy goat gruff. "I need to get to the meadow."

How many butterflies can you see?

For more practice turn to page 34

Well done!

Counting to 10

Now your child can confidently count to 5, practise counting to 10. Ask your child to count the items on this page with you. Point to each one as you count.

"Stop!" growled the troll. "I'm going to eat you for my dinner!"

"Alright," said the brave little billy goat gruff. "But perhaps you should wait until my brother comes along – he's MUCH bigger than me."

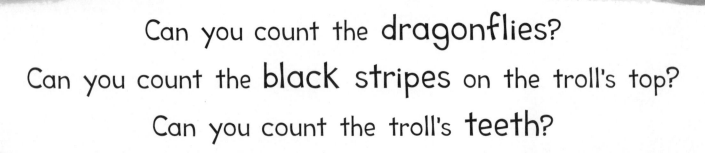

Can you count the **dragonflies?**

Can you count the **black stripes** on the troll's top?

Can you count the troll's **teeth?**

The troll thought this over. Then, with a frown, he allowed the little goat to jump into the meadow.

Can you count the **flowers**?

Can you count the **bricks** on the bridge?

For more practice turn to page 36

Well done!

6–10: Draw around and count

Ask your child to draw a circle around each type of item one at a time as they count aloud. Make sure that the number they say corresponds with the number they are circling.

Next, the medium-sized billy goat gruff set off across the bridge.

"STOP RIGHT THERE!" the troll yelled, jumping out. "Who is trip-trapping over MY BRIDGE?"

Can you count the **trees?**

Can you count the **bees?**

Can you count the **flowers?**

"It's just me, looking for tasty grass to eat,"
said the medium-sized billy goat gruff.

"But I want you for my dinner,"
said the troll.

Can you count the **spots** on the goat's back?

Can you count the **rabbits**?

For more practice turn to page 38
Well done!

19

6–10: How many are there?

Ask your child to count each item, pointing to each one as they go, and then to tell you how many there are. Show them how to write the numerals in the boxes so they start to recognize them, then help them to practice writing the numerals by themselves.

"Alright, but you might want to wait for my big brother – he'll make a much better meal," said the medium-sized billy goat gruff.

How many **bushes?**

How many **lambs?**

How many **flowers?**

The greedy troll licked his lips. Then, with a scowl, he let the medium-sized goat pass. With a hop and a skip, he jumped into the meadow to join his little brother.

How many **beetles?**

How many **worms?**

Can you find any other things to count?

For more practice turn to page 40

Well done!

21

6–10: Same number, looks different

Now the troll started to worry. He wondered how big the biggest billy goat gruff was. He thought about all the other things he could eat for dinner instead!

How many **lambs?**

How many **lambs?**

How many **frogs?**

How many **frogs?**

How many rabbits?

How many rabbits?

How many mice?

How many mice?

How many chicks?

How many chicks?

But goat was still his favourite!

For more practice turn to page 42

Well done!

23

6–10: Which are the same?

At last the big billy goat gruff clattered over the wooden bridge. Out jumped the troll.

"Who is TRIP-TRAPPING over MY BRIDGE? I'll eat you for DINNER!" he roared.

"ME!" answered the big billy goat gruff.
"I'm going to the meadow. Get out of my way!"

He lowered his head, and... BIFF! Up went the troll high into the air and into the river – SPLASH!

6 7 8 9 10

Encourage your child to count the items in each group on the left, and draw a line to the matching group of items on the right. Help them to write the correct number in each box.

How many grey feathers do I have?

For more practice turn to page 44

Well done!

25

Putting it all together

Ask your child to independently count the items and write down how many there are in the boxes provided.

After that, the three billy goats gruff lived happily ever after in the meadow. And they were never bothered by trolls again!

How many leaves?

How many clouds?

How many rabbits?

How many flowers?

How many
trees?

How many
birds?

How many
bees?

How many
mountains?

How many
goats?

How many
butterflies?

For more practice turn to page 46

Well done!

27

Counting in order to 5

How many goats?

Point to each of us as you count us.

How many trees?

How many flowers?

How many **trolls?**

How many **butterflies?**

Well done!

1–5: Draw around and count

Trace the dotted lines. Count each item aloud as you draw around it.

How many **birds**?

How many **leaves**?

How many **snails**?

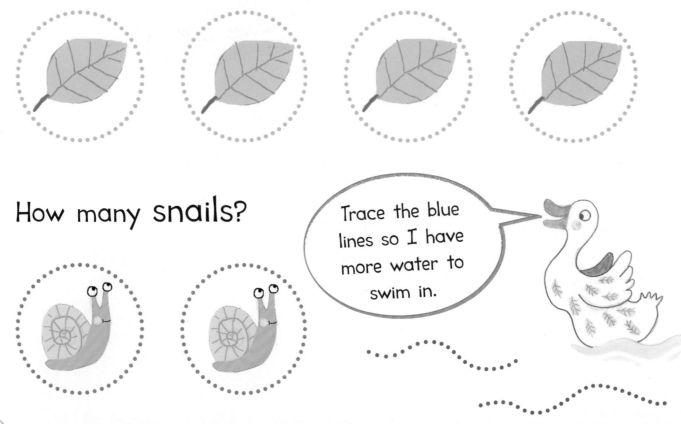

Trace the blue lines so I have more water to swim in.

How many **dragonflies?**

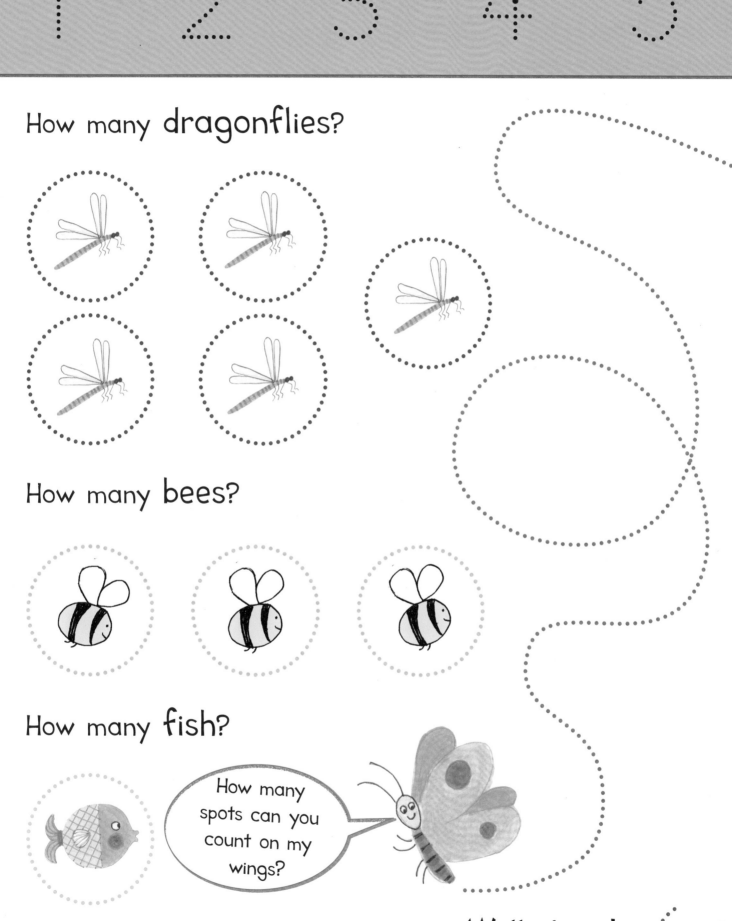

How many **bees?**

How many **fish?**

How many spots can you count on my wings?

Well done!

1–5: How many are there?

Point to each item as you count it. Then trace or write the numbers in the boxes.

How many **lilypads?**

How many **trees?**

How many **rabbits?**

How many **chicks?** ▢

How many **trolls?** ▢

How many **horns do I have?**

How many **frogs?** ▢

Well done! 33

1-5: Same number, looks different

Count the first set and write the number in the box. How many are in the second set? Count them to see if you're right, and write the number in the box.

How many **clouds?**

How many **clouds?**

How many **birds?**

How many **birds?**

 How many **dragonflies?**

 How many **dragonflies?**

How many **apples?**

How many **apples?**

 How many **beetles?**

 How many **beetles?**

Well done!

Counting to 10

Remember to point to each item as you count it.

How many **bees?**

How many **clouds?**

How many **flowers?**

How many **trees?**

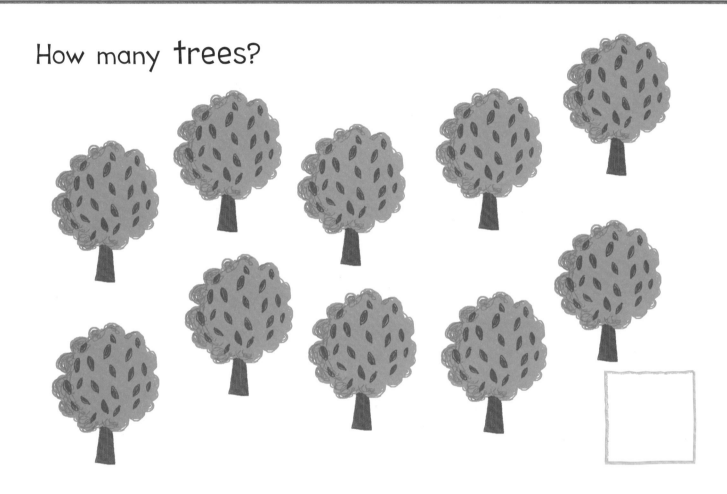

How many **butterflies?**

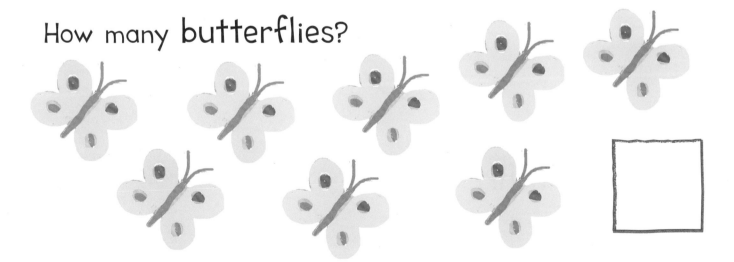

Well done!

37

6–10: Draw around and count

Trace the dotted lines, counting aloud as you complete each circle.

How many **bees?**

How many **bells?**

Can you count my spots?

How many **fish?**

How many **rain drops?**

How many **birds?**

How many **snails?**

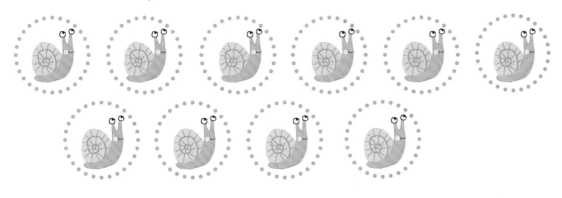

Well done!

39

6–10: How many are there?

Point to each item as you count it. Then trace or write the numbers in the boxes.

How many butterflies?

How many fish?

6 7 8 9 10

How many **lilypads?**

How many **leaves?**

How many **rocks?**

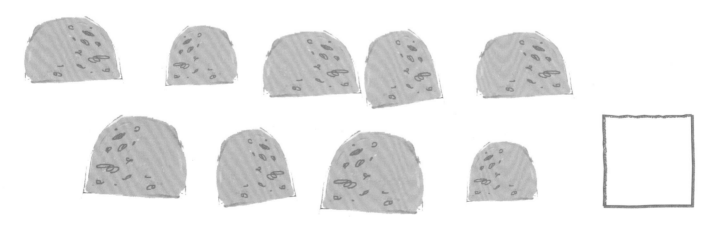

Well done!

41

6–10: Same number, looks different

Count the first set and write the number in the box. How many are in the second set? Count them to see if you're right, and write the number in the box.

 How many mice?

 How many mice?

 How many frogs?

 How many frogs?

6 7 8 9 10

How many **rabbits?**

How many **rabbits?**

How many **chicks?**

How many **chicks?**

Well done!

6–10: Which are the same?

Let's practise that some more!

How many **ducks?**

How many **ducks?**

How many **butterflies?**

How many **butterflies?**

How many **beetles?**

How many **beetles?**

There's no WAY I'm eating worms!

How many **worms?**

How many **worms?**

Well done!

45

Putting it all together

Count the items and write the correct numbers in the boxes.

How many trees?

How many snails?

How many rabbits?

How many flowers?

1 2 3 4 5 6 7 8 9 10

How many
bees?

How many
mountains?

How many
goats?

How many
butterflies?

Well done!

Let's start practising!

1
2
3
4
5
6
7
8
9
10

Exploring Numbers

...with the Elves and the Shoemaker!

Draw along the dotted lines.

Introduction

Exploring numbers from one to ten

Once children have mastered counting to ten, they then need to explore the numbers one to ten and really get to know them.

- At this stage, children need to develop an understanding of the relative size of the numbers – for example, 4 is greater than 2 and less than 7. They also need to be able to tell you how a number can be made – for example, 5 can be made from 1 and 4, and from 2 and 3.

- In the course of completing the activities in this book, your child will need to find pairs of numbers to make a 'focus number'. Encourage them to find all possibilities – for example, 4 can be made by adding 1 and 3, or by adding 2 and 2.

- The activities in this book encourage children to make a focus number by adding two numbers, but many of the focus numbers can be made by adding three or more numbers. For example, 5 can be made by adding 1 and 1 and 3. If you think your child could explore this, let them have a go away from the book.

- The number zero is not explored in this book, but it's still correct if your child includes it as a way of making a focus number. For example, 2 can be made by adding 2 and 0.

STORY TEXT
keeps your child engaged and makes learning and practising fun

INSTRUCTION TEXT
explains what your child will be learning on each spread and how to approach the activities

ACTIVITIES
guide your child through the process of exploring numbers, step by step

DOTTED LINES
to trace throughout help to improve pen control

Number se

Ask your child to po
to all the things in the pic
show seven. Use these as cl
your child think of one way to
write the numbers in the boxes.
the correct symbols in the circles
to tell you all the numbers tha
seven and to say full sen
example, "Six is
than seven."

Can you find on
way to make 7?

62

Numbe

Find a way

ILLUSTRATIONS
contain clues to help your child complete the activities. Look for the clues together and encourage your child to count out loud as they point

84

At midnight, two little elves crept in. They were dressed all in rags. As the shoemaker watched, they began to stitch, sew, and hammer.

1 2 3 4 5 6 7 8 9 10

When all the leather was stitched into beautiful shoes the elves ran away into the night.

Can you write the **correct symbols** in the circles?

7 ◯ 3   7 ◯ 9

Can you draw a circle around each of the things that show seven?

For more practice turn to page 84

Well done! 63

For more practice turn to page 84

NUMBER TRACK can be used to help your child decide whether one number is greater or less than another. If they have to move their finger left on the track from the first number to the second, then the first number is greater; if they have to move their finger right it is less. It's good practice for your child to trace the numerals, too

en

Find a way to make 7.

7

7.

Find a way to make 7.

7

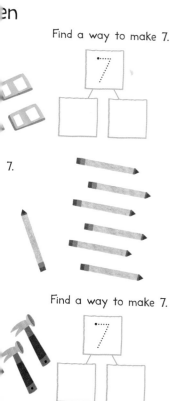

1 2 3 4 5 6 7 8 9 10

7 ◯ 3

Can you trace the correct symbols in the circles?

☐ buttons

☐ cakes

☐ balls of wool

☐ rings

Tick the boxes of all the things that show 7.

7 ◯ 9

☐ birds

Well done! 85

SQUARE BOXES are for numbers; ROUND BOXES are for symbols

CHARACTER SPEECH provides extra activities, tips and guidance

TICKS for your child to trace when they complete each spread provide an extra sense of achievement

51

Numbers one and two

Ask your child to point to all the things on the table that show one. Help them to write the correct symbol in the circle. Do the same on the opposite page for the number two. Help them to write the correct numbers in the boxes.

Once upon a time there was a poor shoemaker. There came a day when he could only buy enough leather to make one more pair of shoes.

Can you draw a circle around each of the things on this table that show one?

> means *more than*
< means *less than*

Can you write the **correct** symbol in the circle?

1  2

For more practice turn to page 72

That night, he cut the leather to the right size and then went to bed. In the morning, he was amazed to find the shoes finished – they were beautiful!

How can we make 2?

2

Can you draw a circle around each of the things on this table that show two?

Can you write the **correct symbols** in the circles?

3 > 2

2 < 4

For more practice turn to page 74

Well done!

53

Number three

Ask your child to point to all the things that show three. Help them to write the correct numbers in the boxes. Then help them to write the correct symbols in the circles.

The shoemaker put the shoes in the shop window. At once a customer came in and bought them. She paid a very good price.

Can you find one way to make 3?

3

Can you draw a circle around each of the things that show three?

With the money, the shoemaker bought enough leather to make two more pairs of shoes.

Can you write the **correct symbols** in the circles?

3 ◯ 5   3 ◯ 2

For more practice turn to page 76

Well done!

Number four

Ask your child to point to all the things in the picture that show four. Use these as clues to help your child think of one way to make four and write the numbers in the boxes. Help them write the correct symbols in the circles.

The shoemaker woke in the morning to find the two pairs of shoes already made – and every bit as fine as the first pair. Customers were waiting outside – they had heard about the beautiful shoes.

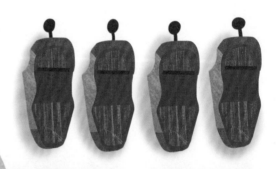

Can you find one way to make 4?

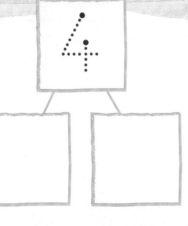

Can you draw a circle around each of the things that show four?

56

The two new pairs sold quickly, and the shoemaker bought enough leather to make four more pairs of shoes.

Can you write the **correct symbols** in the circles?

4 ◯ 2

4 ◯ 5

For more practice turn to page 78

Well done!

Number five

The next day, four pairs of shoes were ready and waiting. And so it went on, day after day.

Can you find one way to make 5?

Can you draw a circle around each of the things that show five?

58

Can you write the **correct symbols** in the circles?

5 ◯ 6

5 ◯ 1

For more practice turn to page 80

Well done! ✓

Number six

Ask your child to point to all the things in the pictures that show six. Use these as clues to help your child think of one way to make six and write the numbers in the boxes. Help them write the correct symbols in the circles.

That night, the shoemaker decided to find out who was helping him. He hid, and waited.

Can you draw a circle around each of the things that show six on this page?

Can you write the **correct symbols** in the circles?

6 ◯ 3   6 ◯ 8

Can you find one way to make 6?

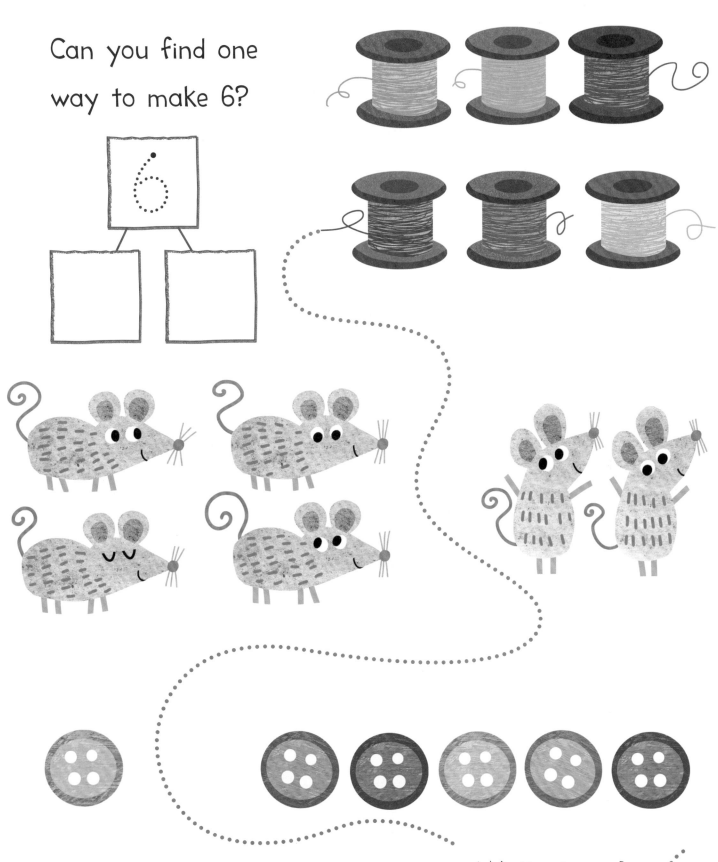

6

For more practice turn to page 82

Well done!

Number seven

At midnight, two little elves crept in. They were dressed all in rags. As the shoemaker watched, they began to stitch, sew, and hammer.

Can you find one way to make 7?

When all the leather was stitched into beautiful shoes the elves ran away into the night.

Can you write the **correct** symbols in the circles?

7 ◯ 3   7 ◯ 9

Can you draw a circle around each of the things that show seven?

For more practice turn to page 84
Well done!

Number eight

The shoemaker thought he must find a way to thank the elves for their help. So in the morning he set to work, making new little clothes, and tiny pairs of shoes.

Can you draw a circle around each of the things on the table that show eight?

Can you write the **correct symbols** in the circles?

8 ◯ 10   8 ◯ 3

Can you find one way to make 8?

8

For more practice turn to page 86

Well done!

Number nine

Ask your child to point to all the things in the picture that show nine. Use these as clues to help your child think of one way to make nine and write the numbers in the boxes. Help them write the correct symbols in the circles. Encourage them to tell you all the numbers that are less than nine, using full sentences.

A few nights later, when everything was ready, the shoemaker laid the presents out on his workbench and hid.

Can you find one way to make 9?

Can you draw a circle around each of the things that show nine?

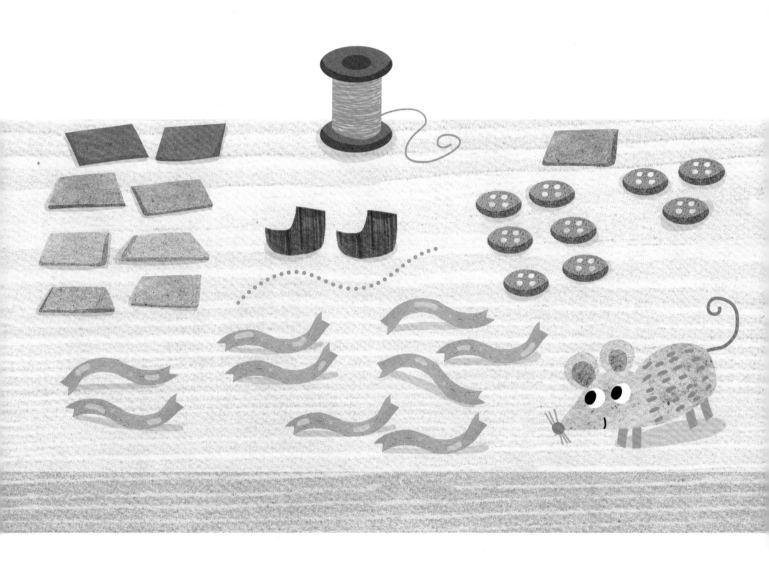

Can you write the **correct symbols** in the circles?

9 ◯ 4   9 ◯ 10

For more practice turn to page 88

Well done!

67

Number ten

When the elves saw the clothes they put them on at once, and danced about with glee. Then they ran away, out of the shop into the night.

Can you find one way to make 10?

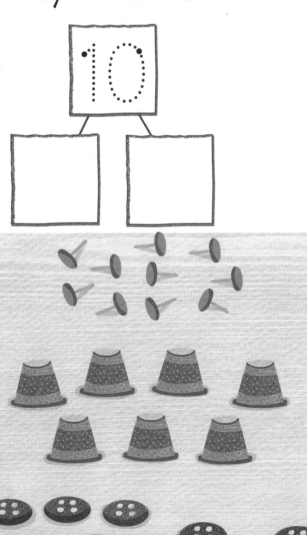

Can you write the **correct symbols** in the circles?

10 ◯ 12   10 ◯ 4

Can you draw a circle around each of the things that show ten?

For more practice turn to page 90 Well done!

69

How many?

Ask your child to count how many items there are and to write the appropriate numerals in the boxes.

After that night, the shoemaker never saw the elves again. But from then on, he had good luck in all that he did.

How many cakes?

How many coins?

How many flowers?

How many cats?

How many people? ☐

How many spots? ☐

How many balls of wool? ☐

How many bows? ☐

How many shoes? ☐

How many mice? ☐

For more practice turn to page 92

Well done!

71

Number one

Tick the boxes of all the things on the table that show 1.

☐ lamps

☐ hammers

☐ boxes

☐ boots

☐ cotton reels

Trace the dotted lines to draw the **symbols.**

`>` means **more than**   `<` means **less than**

Trace the correct symbols in the circles below.

buckles

elves

needles

socks

envelopes

2 > 1   1 < 2

Well done!

73

Number two

Tick the boxes of all the things that show 2.

buttons

flowers

socks

Can you trace the correct symbols in the circles?

ribbons

birds

2 > 1

bows

74

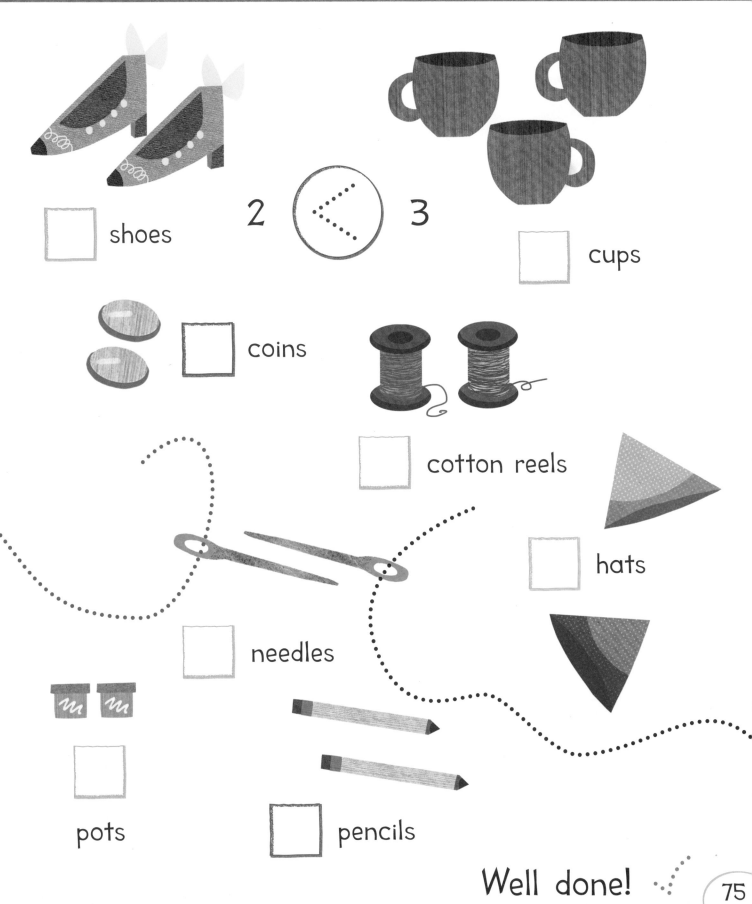

shoes

2 < 3

cups

coins

cotton reels

hats

needles

pots

pencils

Well done!

Number three

Tick the boxes of all the things that show 3.

Can you trace the correct symbols in the circles?

☐ cats

☐ balls of wool

2 ❮ 3

☐ scissors

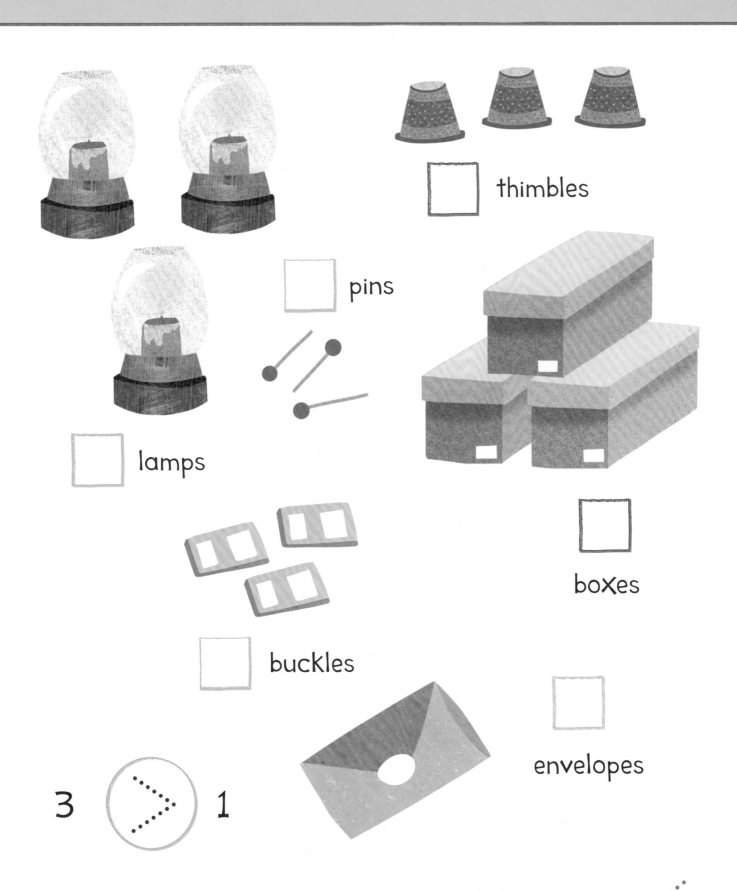

thimbles

pins

lamps

boxes

buckles

envelopes

3 > 1

Well done! ✓

Number four

☐ cakes

☐ coins

☐ birds

☐ flowers

Tick the boxes of all the things that show 4.

 ☐

tacks

3 < 4

☐ shoes

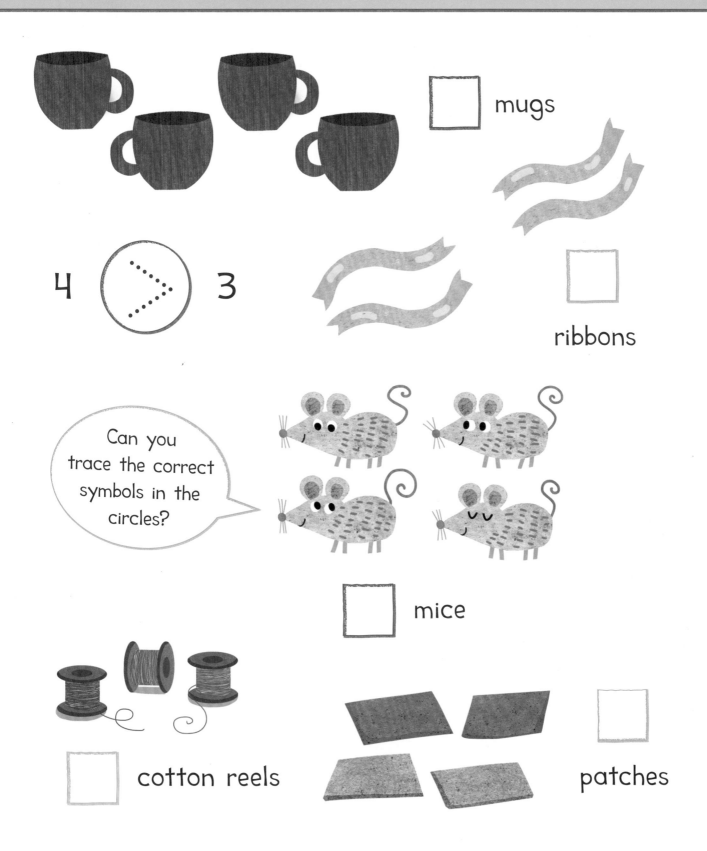

mugs

4 > 3

ribbons

Can you trace the correct symbols in the circles?

mice

cotton reels

patches

Well done!

Number five

rolls of cloth

cotton reels

buttons

pins

ribbons

Tick the boxes of all the things that show 5.

80

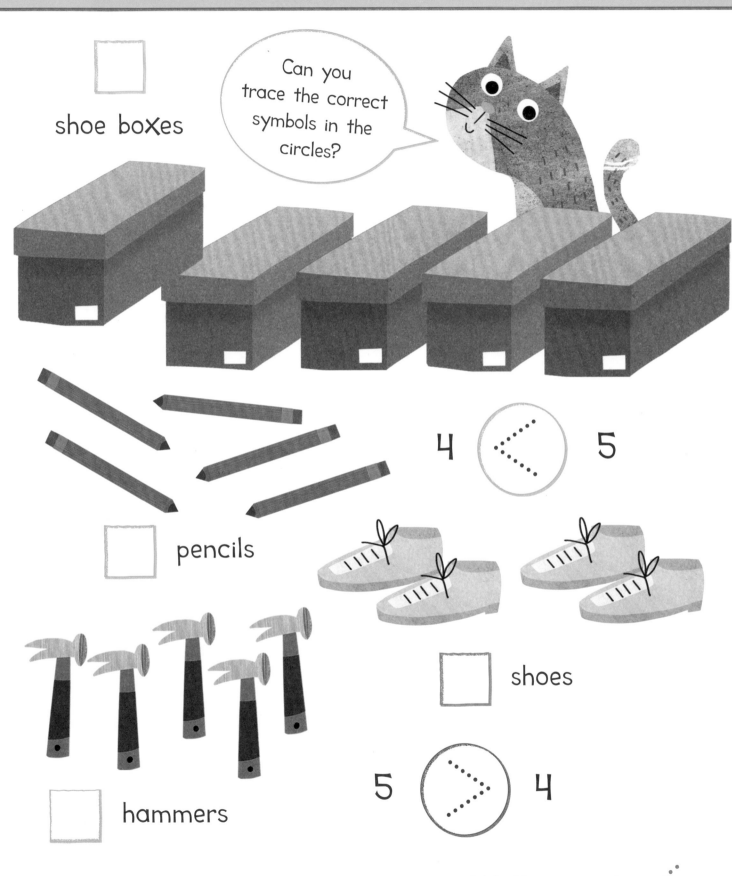

☐ shoe boxes

Can you trace the correct symbols in the circles?

☐ pencils

4 < 5

☐ hammers

☐ shoes

5 > 4

Well done!

Number six

boots

Tick the boxes of all the things that show 6.

6 > 3

coins

buttons

6 < 8

tacks

Can you trace the correct symbols in the circles?

82

Find a way to make 6.

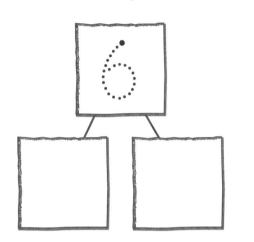

Find a way to make 6.

Find a way to make 6.

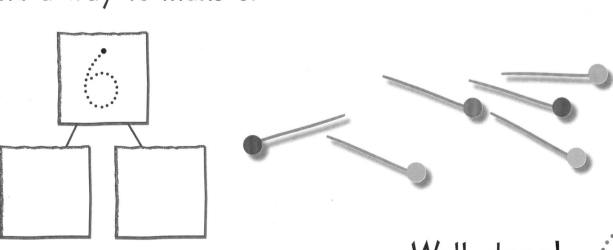

Well done!

Number seven

Find a way to make 7.

Find a way to make 7.

Find a way to make 7.

7 > 3

Can you trace the correct symbols in the circles?

buttons

birds

cakes

Tick the boxes of all the things that show 7.

balls of wool

rings

7 < 9

Well done!

85

Number eight

Tick the boxes of all the things that show 8.

☐ buttons

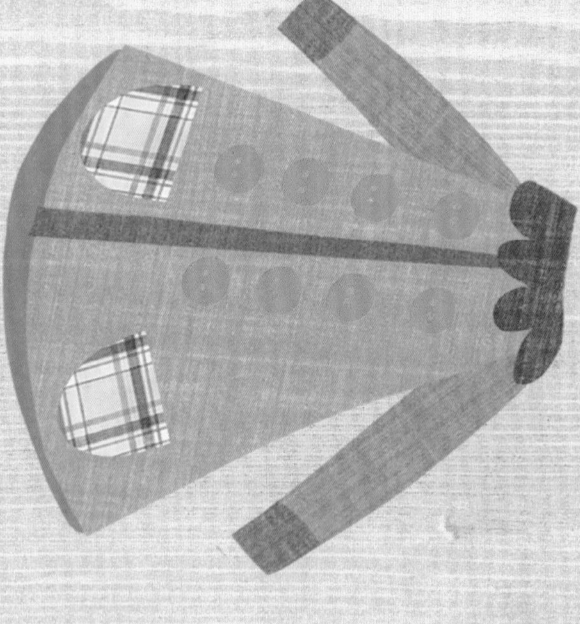

☐ socks

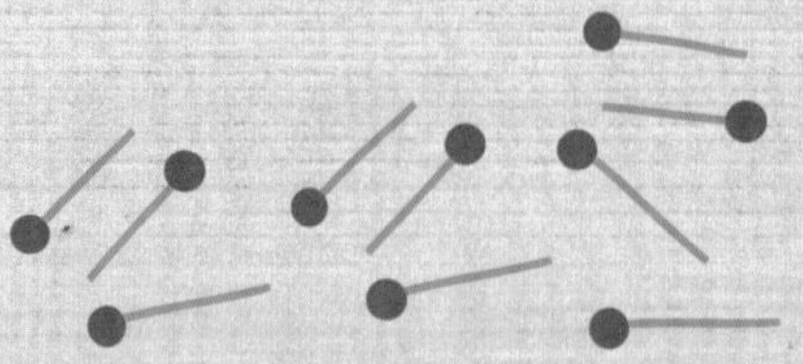

☐ pins

Can you write the **correct symbols** in the circles?

8 ◯ 10   8 ◯ 3

Find a way to make 8.

Find a way to make 8.

Find a way to make 8.

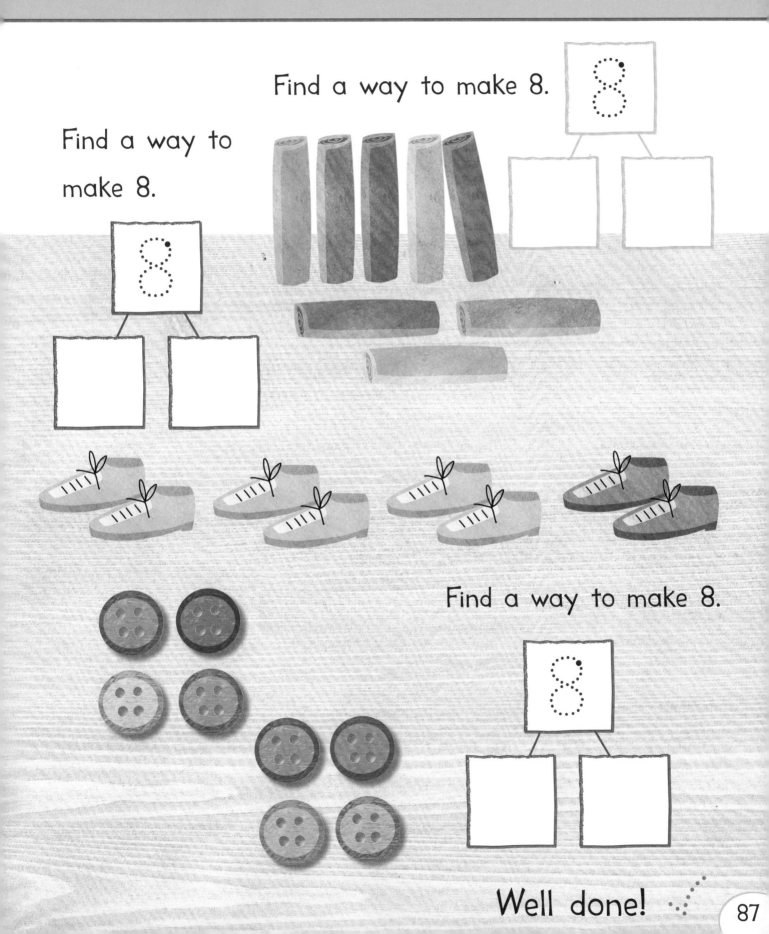

Well done!

Number nine

Find a way to make 9.

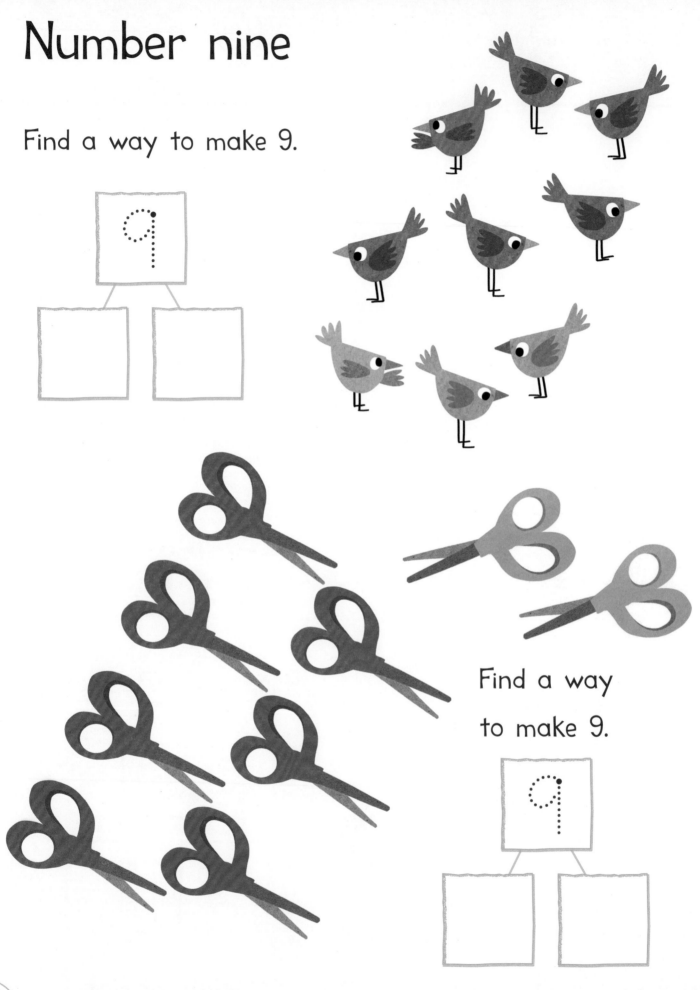

Find a way
to make 9.

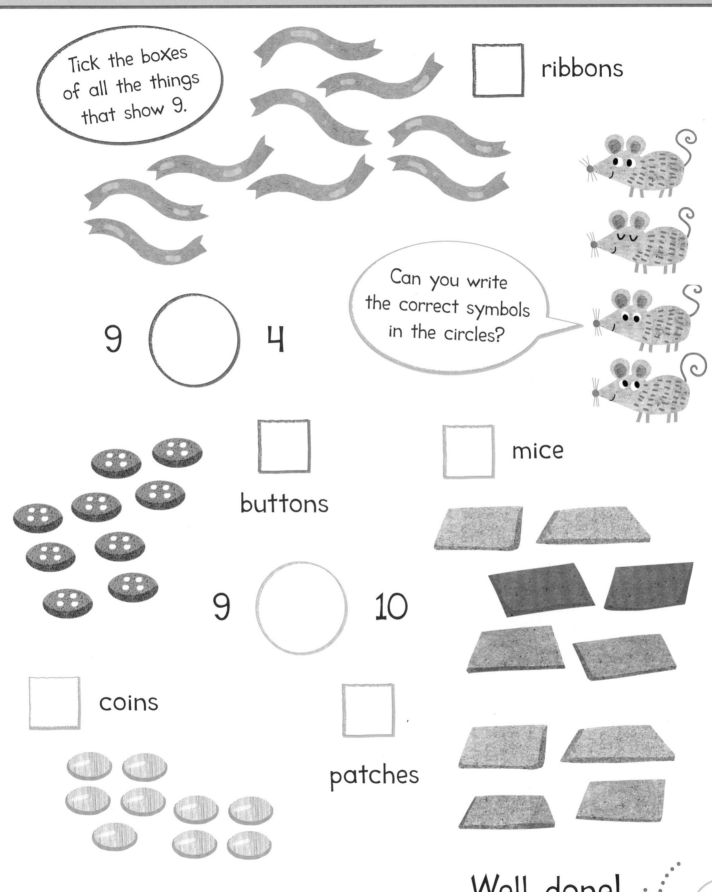

Tick the boxes of all the things that show 9.

☐ ribbons

9 ◯ 4

Can you write the correct symbols in the circles?

☐ mice

☐ buttons

9 ◯ 10

☐ coins

☐ patches

Well done!

89

Number ten

Find a way to make 10.

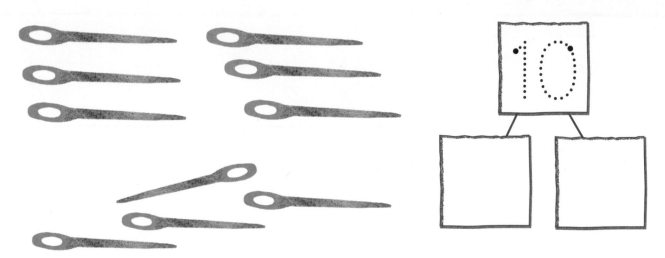

Find a way to make 10.

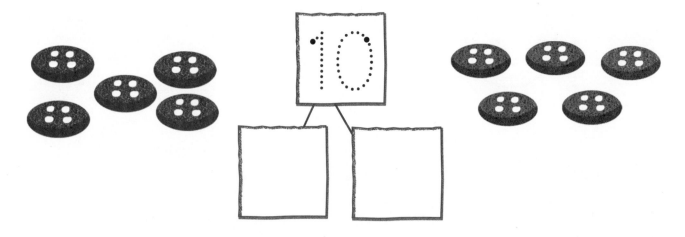

Find a way to make 10.

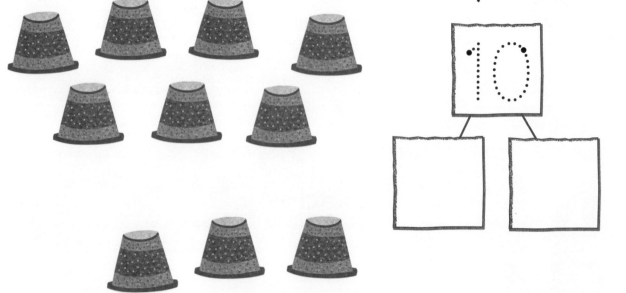

Can you write the **correct symbols** in the circles?

10 ◯ 12

10 ◯ 4

☐ mice

☐ boxes

☐ flowers

Tick the boxes of all the things that show 10.

☐ pins

☐ cakes

Well done!

How many?

How many
birds?

How many
mice?

How many
needles?

How many
lamps?

How many
cotton reels? ☐

How many
buttons? ☐

How many
pencils? ☐

How many
shoes? ☐

Well done!

How many?

How many needles?

How many hammers?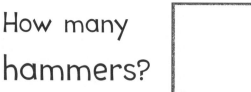

How many buckles?

How many cotton reels?

 How many ribbons?

How many **tacks?**

How many **thimbles?**

How many **buttons?**

How many **people?**

How many **cakes?**

Well done! ✓

95

WELL DONE!

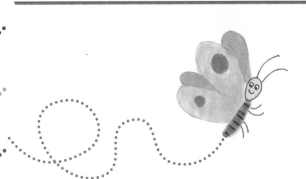

You've finished
Numbers 1–10

Write your name here

Now you know lots of things about the numbers 1 to 10!

Hurrah! Is it time for a nap?